PEANUT BUTTER

Cookbook

Printed in the USA by G&R Publishing Co., Waverly, IA

Published and distributed by:

507 Industrial Street
Waverly, IA 50677

Peanut Butter Cookbook - 101 Recipes with Peanut Butter
ISBN 1-56383-160-0
Item #3719

Appetizers

Ants On A Log

8 celery stalks, cut into 3 to 4" pieces   1/2 C. raisins or chocolate chips
1 C. peanut butter

Fill celery stalks with peanut butter. Place raisins on peanut butter to resemble ants.

Peanut Butter Bread

1 3/4 C. sifted flour
1 tsp. soda
1/2 tsp. salt
1 C. brown sugar

1/2 C. peanut butter
1 egg, beaten
1/2 tsp. maple flavoring
1 C. buttermilk

Sift flour, soda and salt together. Cream brown sugar and peanut butter. Add well beaten egg and stir in flavoring. Add flour mixture alternately with buttermilk and blend well. Bake in a greased loaf pan at 350° for 50 minutes. Cool to lukewarm before slicing.

Peanut Butter Muffins

2 C. sifted all-purpose flour
1 T. baking powder
1 C. milk
2 eggs

1/2 C. sugar
1/2 C. peanut butter
1 tsp. salt

Preheat oven to 400°. In bowl, stir together flour and baking powder, set aside. Place milk, eggs, sugar, peanut butter and salt in blender. Cover and blend to combine. Pour over dry ingredients; stir just to moisten. Fill greased muffin pans 2/3 full. Bake in a 400° oven for 15 to 20 minutes.

Caramel Peanut Butter Dip

30 caramels
1 to 2 T. water
1/4 C. plus 2 T. creamy peanut butter

1/4 C. finely crushed peanuts,
  optional
Sliced apples

In a microwave-safe bowl, microwave the caramels and water on high for 1 minute. Stir. Microwave 1 minute more or until smooth. Add peanut butter and mix well. Microwave for 30 seconds or until smooth. Stir in peanuts, if desired. Serve warm with apples.

Peanut Butter Whip

1/2 C. creamy peanut butter
1/2 C. light whipped topping

1-8 oz. carton light vanilla yogurt

Whip all together. Makes 8 servings. Use on fruit, crackers, bread, etc.

Puppy Chow

1 C. chocolate chips
1 C. peanut butter
1 stick margarine

1-12.3 oz. box Crispix cereal
3 C. powdered sugar

Melt together first three ingredients. Pour over cereal and mix. Pour mixture in paper sack with powdered sugar. Shake well. Keep in airtight container.

Nut and Honey Cream Cheese Spread

1-8 oz. pkg. cream cheese, softened   1 tsp. honey
1/2 C. chunky peanut butter   1/2 tsp. cinnamon

In a medium bowl, combine cream cheese, peanut butter, honey and cinnamon. Spread on graham crackers, bagel chips, whole wheat toast or apple slices. Serve immediately or put in a covered container and refrigerate for up to one week.

Peanut Butter Party Mix

2 T. butter
1/3 C. creamy peanut butter
2 C. Wheat Chex cereal

2 C. Rice Chex cereal
1/4 C. dry roasted peanuts

Melt butter and then add peanut butter; stir until mixed well. Toss cereals and nuts in peanut butter mixture until coated. Remove from heat. Spread on ungreased cookie sheet. Bake at 375° for 8 minutes or until golden brown. Drain on paper towels.

Peanut Butter 'n Jelly Mini Muffins

1 C. flour
1/3 C. packed brown sugar
1 tsp. baking powder
1/2 tsp. baking soda
1/4 tsp. salt

2 eggs
1/2 C. vanilla yogurt
3 T. creamy peanut butter
2 T. vegetable oil
3 T. strawberry or grape jelly

In a large bowl, combine the flour, brown sugar, baking powder, baking soda and salt. In a small mixing bowl, beat the eggs, yogurt, peanut butter and oil on low speed until smooth. Stir into the dry ingredients just until moistened. Fill greased or paper-lined miniature muffin cups half full. Top each with 1/4 teaspoon jelly and remaining batter. Bake at 400° for 10 to 12 minutes or until golden brown. Cool for 5 minutes before removing. Muffins may be baked in regular-size muffin cups for 16 to 18 minutes. Use 3/4 teaspoon jelly on each.

Peanut-Chip-Banana Bread

2 1/2 C. all-purpose flour
1/2 C. sugar
1/2 C. brown sugar, packed
1 T. baking powder
3/4 tsp. salt
1/4 tsp. ground cinnamon
1 C. mashed ripe bananas
   (2 to 3 medium)

1 C. milk
3/4 C. chunky peanut butter
1 egg
3 T. vegetable oil
1 tsp. vanilla extract
1 C. (6 oz.) miniature semisweet
   chocolate chips

In mixing bowl, combine the first six ingredients. Combine bananas, milk, peanut butter, egg, oil and vanilla; mix well. Stir into flour mixture just until combined. Add chocolate chips. Spoon into two greased 8x4x2" loaf pan. Bake at 350° for 50 to 55 minutes or until bread tests done. Cool in pans for 10 minutes before removing to a wire rack. When completely cooled, wrap each loaf in foil and refrigerate overnight.

(continued on next page)

FROSTING:

3 T. chunky peanut butter

2 T. butter or margarine

1 C. confectioners' sugar

1 T. milk

1 tsp. vanilla extract

Chopped peanuts and additional
miniature chocolate chips

The next day, melt peanut butter and butter in a small saucepan; remove from the heat. Stir in confectioners' sugar, milk and vanilla. Frost loaves; sprinkle with nuts and chocolate chips, if desired.

Three-Grain Peanut Butter

1 C. flour
1/2 C. quick-cooking oats
1/2 C. yellow cornmeal
1/2 C. nonfat dry milk powder
1/2 C. sugar

1 T. baking powder
1/2 tsp. salt
2/3 C. peanut butter
1 egg
1 1/2 C. low-fat milk

Mix first seven dry ingredients in bowl. Cut in peanut butter until crumbly. Beat egg and milk in small bowl. Pour into crumb mixture, mix well. Pour into greased loaf pan. Bake at 325° for 1 hour and 10 minutes or until bread tests done. Cool in pan for 10 minutes. Remove to wire rack to cool completely.

Peanut Butter Popcorn

Pop 3/4 cup popcorn kernels.

BOIL TOGETHER 2 MINUTES:
1 C. sugar
1/2 C. honey
1/2 C. corn syrup

ADD:
1 tsp. vanilla
1 C. peanut butter

Pour mixture over popped popcorn and mix well. Put in turkey roaster and bake for 15 minutes at 200°, then stir and put in oven for another 15 minutes.

Main Dish

Szechuan Noodles with Peanut Sauce

12 oz. spaghetti
1/3 C. hot water
1/3 C. smooth peanut butter
2 tsp. soy sauce
2 tsp. white wine vinegar

2 scallions, chopped
2 cloves garlic, minced
1 tsp. honey
1/4 tsp. hot red pepper flakes

Cook the pasta as directed on package. In a medium bowl, blend water and peanut butter with a whisk. Stir in soy sauce, vinegar, garlic, honey, hot pepper flakes and all but 1 tablespoon chopped scallions. Combine the sauce with pasta and serve hot. Garnish with the reserved scallions.

Peanut Butter Pancakes

1 C. pancake mix
2 T. sugar
1 egg

1/3 C. peanut butter
1-5 oz. can evaporated milk
1/3 C. water

In a bowl combine pancake mix and sugar. In a small bowl, beat egg and peanut butter; add milk and water. Stir into dry ingredients just until moistened. Pour batter by 1/4 cupfuls onto a lightly greased medium-hot griddle. Turn when bubbles form on top of pancakes; cook until second side is golden brown.

HONEY BUTTER:
1/4 C. butter, no substitutes, softened   2 T. honey

Combine in small bowl and serve with pancakes.

Baked Peanut Butter Chicken

1 egg, beaten
1/2 C. mayonnaise
1 tsp. salt
Wheat germ

1/2 C. peanut butter
1 T. milk
6 pieces chicken, skinned

Mix peanut butter, mayonnaise, milk and salt with beaten egg. Dip chicken pieces into mixture. Roll in wheat germ and place in greased baking dish. Bake at 350° for 1 hour.

Crispy Chicken & Honey Dipping Sauce

1 C. salad dressing
1/4 C. honey
2 T. Dijon mustard
2 T. peanut butter

4 boneless, skinless chicken
   breasts, cut into strips
1 1/2 C. finely crushed potato chips

Mix dressing, honey, mustard and peanut butter. Brush chicken with 1/2 cup of the dressing mixture; coat with crushed chips. Place on greased cookie sheet. Bake at 425° for 7 to 9 minutes. Turn, continue baking 4 to 5 minutes or until lightly browned. Serve with remaining dressing mixture as a dipping sauce.

Peanut Chicken

3 lbs. lean chicken breasts
1/2 tsp. five spice powder
1-8 oz. pkg. snow peas
1/4 C. corn flour
1 C. peanut oil

1 C. raw peanuts
1 tsp. crushed garlic
1 tsp. finely grated ginger
2 T. creamy peanut butter
1/2 C. chicken stock
2 T. soy sauce

Cut the chicken into serving pieces. Rub the chicken pieces with five spice powder, put them in a heatproof dish and place on a rack in wok. Pour water into wok to come below level of rack, cover and steam chicken for 35 to 45 minutes. Coat the chicken pieces with corn flour. Pour off water from wok, heat wok until it is quite dry and add the cup of oil. Heat, then fry the peanuts on medium-low heat, stirring until they are golden brown. Remove on slotted spoon and drain on absorbent paper. Fry chicken pieces a few at a time, until golden brown on both sides. As each batch is browned, remove to

(continued on next page)

a plate and keep warm. Pour all but 1 tablespoon of oil from wok and on low heat fry garlic and ginger, stirring constantly. Add snow peas and stir-fry for 2 minutes or until color brightens and vegetables are tender, but still crisp. Add peanut butter, chicken stock and soy sauce. Bring quickly to a boil, stir in corn flour, mix until it becomes clear. Return chicken and peanuts to wok, stir just to combine and serve immediately with rice.

Peanut Butter French Toast

1/4 C. creamy peanut butter
1 T. butter
2 eggs, slightly beaten

1 C. milk
6 slices bread

Heat in heavy skillet 1 tablespoon of butter. Meanwhile, using a shallow bowl, gradually beat the milk into 1/4 cup creamy peanut butter. As you beat this mixture, add your slightly beaten eggs. When mixture is soupy enough, dip the slices of bread into it. Add two slices to the hot butter in your skillet. Lightly brown on one side and turn with spatula to brown other side. Add more butter if necessary to keep slices from sticking. Continue until all slices have been browned.

Grilled Peanut Butter & Banana

1/2 C. peanut butter
8 slices English muffin bread

2 medium bananas
Butter, softened

Spread peanut butter over 4 bread slices. Slice bananas; arrange on peanut butter. Top with remaining bread. Spread butter over tops of bread. Place sandwiches butter side down in skillet. Spread butter over tops of bread. Cook uncovered over medium heat about 4 minutes or until bottoms are golden brown; turn. Cook 2 to 3 minutes longer or until bottoms are golden brown and peanut butter is melted.

Desserts

Layered Brownies

BROWNIE LAYER:

4-1 oz. squares unsweetened
   chocolate
3/4 C. (1 1/2 sticks) butter
2 C. granulated sugar

3 eggs
1 tsp. vanilla extract
1 C. all-purpose flour
1 C. chopped peanuts

PEANUT BUTTER LAYER:

1 C. peanut butter
1/2 C. confectioners' sugar

1 tsp. vanilla extract

GLAZE:

4-1 oz. squares semisweet chocolate

1/4 C. (1/2 stick) butter

(continued on next page)

BROWNIE LAYER: Preheat oven to 350°. In large microwavable bowl, heat the unsweetened chocolate and butter in microwave on high for 2 minutes, just until the butter is melted. Stir until the chocolate is completely melted. Stir in the granulated sugar. Then mix in the beaten eggs and vanilla until well blended. Stir in the flour and peanuts. Spread in greased 9x13" baking pan. Bake for 30 to 35 minutes or until wooden toothpick inserted in the center comes out with fudgy crumbs. Do not over bake. Cool in the pan.

PEANUT BUTTER LAYER: Combine peanut butter, confectioners' sugar and vanilla in medium-size bowl until well blended and smooth. Spread over the cooled brownies.

GLAZE: Combine semisweet chocolate and butter in a small microwavable bowl and heat in microwave on high for 2 minutes, just until the butter is melted. Stir until the chocolate is completely melted. Spread over the peanut butter layer. Cool until set and then cut into squares.

Chocolate Marshmallow
Mile-High Squares

1-12 oz. pkg. semisweet chocolate
   chips
1-11 oz. pkg. butterscotch chips

1/2 C. peanut butter
1-16 oz. pkg. miniature marshmallows
1 C. dry roasted peanuts

In a large microwave-safe bowl, microwave semisweet chocolate chips, butterscotch chips and peanut butter on medium-high power for 2 minutes, stir. Microwave an additional 10 to 20 second intervals, stirring until smooth. Cool for 1 minute. Stir in marshmallows and peanuts. Spread into a foil-lined 9x13x2" baking pan. Refrigerate until firm. Cut into squares.

Great Big Double-Peanut Cookies

2 1/2 C. flour
1 tsp. baking soda
1/4 tsp. salt
1/2 C. butter or margarine, room temp.
2/3 C. packed brown sugar

1/2 C. white sugar
2 eggs
1 1/2 tsp. vanilla
1 C. creamy peanut butter
2 C. peanut M&M's

Preheat oven to 350°. Combine flour, soda and salt. Reserve. At high speed, beat butter with sugars until fluffy, approximately 2 minutes. Reduce speed to low. Beat in eggs and vanilla until combined. Beat in peanut butter until combined. Gradually beat in flour mixture. Roll 1/4 cupfuls of dough into balls; place 3" apart on ungreased baking sheets. Flatten dough into 3" circles. Press M&M's into cookies. Bake 10 to 12 minutes or until lightly browned and candies begin to crack. Cool 2 minutes. Remove from pans; cool completely on rack.

Chocolate Peanut Butter Parfaits

2 T. skim milk
2 T. peanut butter
1 C. whipped topping

2 C. cold skim milk
1-4 oz. pkg. instant sugar-free
    chocolate flavor pudding

Mix 2 tablespoons milk into peanut butter in small bowl. Stir in whipped topping. Pour 2 cups milk into large bowl. Add pudding mix. Beat with wire whisk, 1 to 2 minutes. Spoon pudding and whipped topping mixture into six parfait glasses. Refrigerate 1 hour or until ready to serve. Garnish with additional whipped topping.

Peanut Butter Snowballs

1 C. powdered sugar
1/2 C. creamy peanut butter

3 T. butter, softened
1 lb. vanilla candy coating

In a mixing bowl, combine sugar, peanut butter and butter, mix well. Shape into 1" balls and place on waxed paper-lined cookie sheet. Chill for 30 minutes or until firm. Melt the candy coating in a microwave-safe bowl. Dip balls and place on waxed paper to harden.

VARIATION: Vanilla candy coating can be sprinkled lightly with finely chopped nuts, cocoa powder or sprinkles before hardening.

Peanut Butter and Jelly Pie

1-8 oz. pkg. cream cheese, softened
1/3 C. peanut butter
1/2 C. confectioners' sugar
1 T. milk

1-9" chocolate flavored pie crust
1/2 C. strawberry preserves or any
  flavor
2 C. whipped topping

In a large bowl, combine the cream cheese and peanut butter, mixing until well blended.
Add the sugar and milk; mix well. Spoon cream cheese mixture into pie crust. Chill.
Spread with the preserves and top with whipped topping.

Chocolate Peanut Butter Balls

1 stick oleo, softened
1 lb. powdered sugar
1-18 oz. jar crunchy peanut butter

3 C. Wheaties, measure then crush
1 lb. chocolate candy coating

Mix above ingredients except chocolate candy coating with a spoon or by hand, then roll into balls the size of a walnut or smaller. Chill. Melt chocolate candy coating in double boiler. Dip balls into melted chocolate and place on waxed paper to cool (Hint: A toothpick works well.) Refrigerate.

Peanut Butter Mallow Candy

2-10 oz. pkgs. peanut butter or
  butterscotch chips
3/4 C. butter (no substitution)
1/2 C. peanut butter

1-10 1/2 oz. pkg. mini-marshmallows
3/4 C. chopped peanuts
3/4 C. flaked coconut

In a microwave or double boiler, heat chips, butter and peanut butter until melted. Add remaining ingredients and mix well. Spread into a lightly greased 15x10x1" baking pan. Refrigerate until firm. Cut into squares.

"Bun" Candy Bars

1 C. milk chocolate chips
1 C. crunchy peanut butter
1 C. butterscotch chips
1/4 C. milk
1/2 C. oleo

2 T. dry vanilla pudding
1/2 tsp. maple flavoring
3 1/4 C. powdered sugar
1 C. dry roasted peanuts

Melt chips and peanut butter and pour half into a greased pan, chill. Cook milk, oleo, pudding and maple flavoring until mixture boils. Add powdered sugar and mix together. Pour mixture over chocolate in pan. To remaining half of chocolate mixture, add peanuts and pour on top of cream layer. Refrigerate, cut and serve. Keep refrigerated.

Oh Henry Bars

1 C. brown sugar
1/2 C. white Karo
1 tsp. salt
1/2 C. peanut butter

1/2 C. butter
1 tsp. vanilla
4 C. oatmeal
1 C. chocolate chips

Cream sugar and butter until fluffy. Add Karo, vanilla, salt and oatmeal. Spread in 9x13" pan. Bake at 350° for 15 minutes. Combine peanut butter and chocolate chips. Spread on hot bars. When chips melt, mix around to blend.

Swirl Cookies

1 roll refrigerated sugar cookies
1 small pkg. butter cream fudge
  frosting mix

3/4 C. chunky-style peanut butter
1 T. butter, softened
2 T. water

Let cookie dough roll soften at room temperature for about 1 hour. Combine frosting mix, peanut butter, butter and water. Stir to form a ball. Roll between two sheets of waxed paper to form 13x10" rectangle. Roll softened cookie dough to form a 13x10" rectangle between two sheets of waxed paper. Remove top sheet of waxed paper. Peel off top waxed paper of chocolate layer and flip onto sugar cookie layer. Peel off waxed paper. Roll up, jellyroll fashion, starting at 13" side. Use bottom waxed paper sheet to guide rolling. Wrap in waxed paper. Refrigerate for at least 1 hour. Cut into 1/4" slices. Place on ungreased cookie sheet, 2" apart. Bake at 375° for 8 to 10 minutes or until edges are lightly browned. Cookies will appear light and puffy in center. Cool on cookie sheets 2 minutes and then remove.

Peanut Butter Brownies

1 C. + 2 T. sugar
1/2 C. peanut butter
1 T. vanilla
1 tsp. baking powder
2 eggs
3/8 C. brown sugar

2 T. margarine
1 1/2 C. whole wheat flour
   or 1 1/2 C. white flour
3/4 tsp. salt
Chopped peanuts, optional

Heat oven to 350°. Combine sugars, peanut butter, margarine and vanilla. Beat and combine eggs. Add dry ingredients. Bake in a 9x13" pan at 350° for 25 to 30 minutes. Sprinkle with chopped peanuts

Peanut Butter Fudge

3 C. sugar	1/3 C. peanut butter
1 large T. corn syrup	1 tsp. vanilla
3/4 C. milk	Chopped nuts, if desired

Stir the sugar, corn syrup and milk together. Cook to the hard ball stage. (Watch carefully as this is likely to burn.) Remove from heat; add the peanut butter and vanilla. Beat until creamy. Pour into a greased 9x13" pan. Nuts may be added, if desired. Score while still warm.

Peanut Crunch Cake

1 pkg. yellow cake mix
1 C. peanut butter
1/2 C. packed brown sugar
1 C. water
3 eggs

1/4 C. vegetable oil
1/2 to 3/4 C. chocolate chips
1/2 to 3/4 C. peanut butter chips
1/2 C. chopped peanuts

In a large mixing bowl, beat cake mix, peanut butter and brown sugar on low speed until crumbly. Set aside 1/2 cup. Add water, eggs and oil to remaining crumb mixture. Blend on low speed until moistened. Beat on high 2 minutes. Stir in 1/4 cup each of the chocolate and peanut butter chips. Pour into greased 9x13" pan. Combine peanuts, reserved crumb mixture and remaining chips. Sprinkle over batter. Bake at 350° for 40 to 45 minutes or until a toothpick inserted in the center comes out clean. Cool completely.

Chocolate Peanut Cookies

1 C. margarine, softened
1 C. creamy peanut butter
1 C. granulated sugar
1 C. packed light brown sugar
2 eggs

2 1/2 C. all-purpose flour
1 1/2 tsp. baking soda
1 tsp. baking powder
1/2 tsp. salt
2 C. chocolate chips

Mix first five ingredients together in an electric mixer on medium speed until well blended. Stir together and add to mixture gradually the last four ingredients. Mix until well blended. Stir in chocolate chips. Drop by rounded teaspoon on greased cookie sheet. Bake at 375° for 8 to 10 minutes.

Dinosaur Dirt Cookies

1/4 C. dirt (cocoa)
2 C. crushed bones (sugar)
2 C. dried grass (oatmeal)

1/2 C. swamp water (water)
1/2 C. fat (butter)
1/2 C. squashed bugs (peanut butter)

Mix the dirt and swamp water. Add bones and fat. Heat to boiling. Add the dry grass. Remove from heat and add the bugs. Mix and spoon onto waxed paper. Let cool and eat.

Oatmeal-Peanut Butter Drops

1/2 C. white sugar
1/2 C. packed brown sugar
1/2 C. margarine
1/2 C. peanut butter
1 egg
1/2 tsp. vanilla

1 C. flour
1/2 tsp. soda
1/4 tsp. baking powder
1/4 tsp. salt
1 1/2 C. quick oatmeal

Mix first six ingredients. Cream together. Stir in remaining ingredients. Drop by teaspoonful about 2" apart. Bake at 375° for 8 to 10 minutes.

Caramel Apple Pizza

1-18 oz. refrigerated sugar
  cookie dough
1-8 oz. cream cheese, softened
1/2 C. peanut butter
1/2 C. brown sugar
2 T. milk

4 C. sliced tart apples
1-12 oz. can 7-Up
1 tsp. cinnamon
1/2 C. caramel ice cream topping
1/3 C. pecans

Press cookie dough into a greased 14" pizza pan. Bake at 350° for 20 minutes. Cool. Loosen from pizza pan. Combine cream cheese, peanut butter, brown sugar and milk, beat until smooth. spread over crust. Combine apples and 7-Up. Soak 5 minutes. Drain well. Toss apples with cinnamon; arrange over cream cheese. Drizzle with caramel topping and sprinkle with pecans.

Peanut Butter Hershey's Kiss Cookies

3 1/2 C. flour
2 tsp. soda
1 C. butter
2/3 C. peanut butter
1 C. sugar

1 C. brown sugar
2 eggs
2 tsp. vanilla
1 pkg. Hershey's kisses

Mix together peanut butter, white and brown sugar, eggs and vanilla. Blend dry ingredients together; then add to the first mixture and mix in. Form into balls, place on cookie sheet and bake for 8 to 10 minutes. Add Hershey's kisses to tops of cookies and bake for 2 to 5 more minutes.

Baby Ruth Bars

1/2 C. sugar
1/2 C. brown sugar
1 1/2 to 2 C. chunky peanut butter
1-12 oz. bag milk chocolate chips

1/2 C. white corn syrup
1/2 C. dark corn syrup
6 C. corn flakes

Bring sugars and syrups to a boil, then add chunky peanut butter and mix. Pour over corn flakes and mix. Put in a buttered 9x13" pan. Melt chocolate chips and spread over top.

Candy Bar Pizza

2 pkgs. ready-made chocolate
   chip cookie dough
1/2 C. chocolate chips

6 T. peanut butter
Assorted candy bars

Press cookie dough into 15x10" pan and bake as directed on package. Remove from oven. Sprinkle chocolate chips over top. Drop peanut butter over that. When shiny, spread over bars. Top with chopped up candy bars.

No Bake Bars

4 C. Cheerios
2 C. crisp rice cereal
2 C. dry roasted peanuts
2 C. M & M's

1 C. light corn syrup
1 C. sugar
1 1/2 C. creamy peanut butter
1 tsp. vanilla extract

In a large bowl, combine the first four ingredients, set aside. In a saucepan, bring corn syrup and sugar to a boil, stirring frequently. Remove from the heat; stir in peanut butter and vanilla. Pour over cereal mixture and toss to coat evenly. Spread into a greased 15x10x1" baking pan. Cool. Cut into 3x3" bars. Yield: 15 bars.

Outrageous Chocolate Chip Cookies

1 C. sugar
2/3 C. brown sugar
1 C. softened butter
2 eggs
1 tsp. vanilla
1 C. peanut butter

2 C. flour
1 C. oats
2 tsp. baking soda
1/2 tsp. salt
1 pkg. mini Hershey's Kisses or
    mini M & M's

Mix together sugar, brown sugar, butter, egg, vanilla and peanut butter. Then mix in flour, oats, baking soda, salt and mini kisses or mini M & M's. Drop dough on ungreased cookie sheet. Bake at 350° for 10 minutes.

Peanut Butter Patties

1 sleeve Ritz or similar crackers   1 block chocolate candy
Peanut butter

Spread crackers with peanut butter to make sandwiches. Melt chocolate in microwave or double boiler. Dip peanut butter sandwiches in chocolate. Place on waxed paper. Cool at room temperature.

Peanut Butter Milk Shake

1/2 C. peanut butter
2 T. sugar

2 tsp. vanilla extract
4 C. cold milk

You will need large drinking container or blender to put in ingredients. Begin by blending or beating in 1/2 cup milk with peanut butter, sugar and vanilla extract until smooth. Take remaining 3 1/2 cups of milk and blend or beat in until you have a nice smooth shake.

Cap'n Crunch Bars

1 3/4 lbs. almond bark
1/2 C. peanut butter
2 C. Cap'n Crunch cereal

2 C. Rice Krispies
2 C. peanuts
2 C. mini-marshmallows

Melt the almond bark in double boiler. Remove from heat and add peanut butter. Mix remaining ingredients in large bowl. Pour bark mixture over and mix. Let stand 3 minutes. Drop on waxed paper or put in jellyroll pan and cut into bars. They harden quite fast.

Snickers Pie

1 graham cracker crust
1/3 C. Grape-Nuts
1/3 C. chunky peanut butter

1 pt. chocolate frozen yogurt
1 pkg. instant chocolate pudding
1-8 oz. whipped topping

Mix all ingredients together. Put in crust and freeze.

Peanut Butter Sundaes

1 C. light corn syrup
1 C. chunky peanut butter

1/4 C. milk
Ice Cream

In a mixing bowl, stir together the corn syrup, peanut butter and milk until well blended. Serve over ice cream. Store in refrigerator.

Chocolate Peanut Butter Ice Cream Sauce

1-11 1/2 oz. pkg. milk chocolate chips   1/3 C. milk
1/4 C. peanut butter

In small saucepan, combine all ingredients. Cook over very low heat, stirring constantly until chocolate melts and mixture is smooth. Serve over ice cream or other desserts. Refrigerate leftovers. Reheat before serving.

Cheerios Treats

5 T. butter or margarine
1-10 oz. pkg. miniature marshmallows
1 C. M & M's

1/2 C. peanut butter
1 C. chocolate covered raisins,
  optional
5 C. Cheerios

Grease 9x13" pan. Microwave margarine in a large bowl on high until melted. Stir in marshmallows and microwave for 1 to 2 minutes or until smooth, stirring halfway through. Stir in peanut butter. Immediately add cereal and candies. Mix lightly until well coated. Press mixture into prepared pan. Cool, cut and serve.

Triple Layer Cookie Bars

1/2 C. margarine
1 1/2 C. graham cracker crumbs
1-7 oz. pkg. flaked coconut

1-14 oz. sweetened condensed milk
1-12 oz. pkg. chocolate chips
1/2 C. creamy peanut butter

Preheat oven to 350°. In a 13x9" baking pan, melt margarine in oven. Sprinkle crumbs evenly over margarine. Top evenly with coconut, then sweetened condensed milk. Bake 25 minutes or until lightly browned. In small saucepan over low heat, melt chocolate chips with peanut butter. Spread evenly over hot coconut layer. Cool 25 minutes. Chill thoroughly. Cut into bars. Store loosely covered at room temperature.

Reese's Chewy Chocolate Cookies

2 C. flour
3/4 C. cocoa
1 tsp. baking soda
1/2 tsp. salt
1 1/4 C. butter or margarine

2 C. sugar
2 eggs
2 tsp. vanilla
1 2/3 C. Reese's peanut butter
   chips

Preheat oven to 350°. In bowl, stir together flour, cocoa, baking soda and salt. In large mixing bowl, beat butter and sugar until light and fluffy. Add eggs and vanilla; beat well. Gradually add flour mixture, beating well. Stir in chips. Drop by teaspoons onto greased cookie sheet. Bake 8 to 9 minutes. (Do not over bake; cookies will be soft.) They will puff while baking and flatten while cooling. Cool slightly; remove from cookie sheet. Cool completely.

Chocolate Peanut Supreme

1/2 C. chunky peanut butter
1/3 C. butter or margarine, melted
1 1/2 C. graham cracker crumbs
1/2 C. sugar

1-5.9 oz. pkg. instant chocolate
  pudding mix
3 C. cold milk
1-12 oz. carton whipped topping, thawed
1 C. chopped peanuts

In a bowl, combine peanut butter and butter. Stir in cracker crumbs and sugar; mix well. Press into a greased 9x13" dish. Prepare pudding with milk according to package directions; spoon over crust. Spread with whipped topping; sprinkle with peanuts. Cover and refrigerate for at least 1 hour or until soft. Refrigerate leftovers.

Peanut Butter Sandwich Cookies

1 pkg. Duncan Hines peanut
  butter cookie mix

1 egg
3-1.55 oz. bars milk chocolate

Preheat oven to 375°. Combine cookie mix contents and peanut butter packet from mix and egg in large bowl. Stir until thoroughly blended. Put tablespoon of cookie dough onto ungreased baking sheet. Bake at 375° for 7 to 9 minutes or until set, but not browned. Cool 1 minute on baking sheet. Cut each milk chocolate bar into 12 sections. To assemble, carefully remove one cookie from baking sheet. Place one milk chocolate section on bottom of warm cookie; top with second cookie. Press together to make a sandwich. Repeat with remaining cookies. Place sandwich cookies on cooling rack until chocolate is set. Store in airtight container.

Peanut Butter Cookie Pops

1/2 C. butter, softened
1/2 C. creamy peanut butter
1/2 C. brown sugar
1/2 C. white sugar
1 egg
1 tsp. vanilla

1 1/2 C. flour
1/2 tsp. baking powder
1/2 tsp. soda
1/4 tsp. salt
12 wooden craft sticks
12 miniature Snickers or Milky Ways

Cream butter, peanut butter and sugars. Beat in egg and vanilla until light and fluffy. Combine dry ingredients; gradually add to creamed mixture. Insert stick in small end of each candy bar. Divide dough into 12 pieces. Wrap 1 piece around each candy bar. Place 4" apart on ungreased baking sheet. Bake at 375° for 14 to 16 minutes until golden brown. Cool 10 minutes; remove from pan to wire rack.

Peanut Butter and Jam Bars

1 C. butter, softened (no substitutions)
1 C. sugar
1/2 C. peanut butter
1 large egg

3 C. flour
1 C. salted dry roasted peanuts,
   coarsely chopped
1 C. grape or strawberry jam

Preheat oven to 350°. Grease 9x13" metal baking pan. Line pan with foil; grease foil. In large bowl with mixer at low speed, beat butter and sugar until mixed. Increase speed to high; beat until light and fluffy. Reduce speed to low; beat in peanut butter, egg until well combined. Beat in flour just until moistened. Beat in peanuts. Reserve 2 cups of dough. Press rest evenly on bottom of pan. Spread jam over dough. Sprinkle reserved dough over jam. Bake 45 to 50 minutes until golden. Cool completely in pan on wire rack. When cool, transfer with foil to cutting board. Cut lengthwise into three strips, then cut each strip crosswise into 8 bars.

Honey-Peanut Butter Cookies

1/2 C. shortening
1 C. creamy peanut butter
1 C. honey
2 eggs, lightly beaten

3 C. all-purpose flour
1 C. sugar
1 1/2 tsp. baking soda
1 tsp. baking powder
1/2 tsp. salt

In a mixing bowl, mix shortening, peanut butter and honey. Add eggs; mix well. Combine flour, sugar, baking soda, baking powder and salt; add to peanut butter mixture and mix well. Roll into 1 to 1 1/2" balls and place on ungreased baking sheet. Flatten with a fork dipped in flour. Bake at 350° for 8 to 10 minutes.

Quick Little Devil's

1-18 1/4 oz. pkg. devil's food
  cake mix
1 C. butter or margarine, melted

1-7 oz. jar marshmallow creme
3/4 C. peanut butter

In a bowl, combine cake mix and butter. Mix well. Set aside 1 cup for topping. Spread remaining cake mixture into a greased 13x9" baking pan. Combine the marshmallow creme and peanut butter. Carefully spread over cake mixture. Crumble reserved cake mixture over the top. Bake at 350° for 18 to 20 minutes or until a toothpick inserted near middle comes out with moist crumbs (do not over bake). Cool completely. Cut into squares.

Peanut Delights

FIRST LAYER:
1 C. flour
1/2 C. dry roasted peanuts
1/2 C. margarine, softened

SECOND LAYER:
1-8 oz. pkg. cream cheese
1 C. whipped topping
1 C. powdered sugar
1/2 C. peanut butter

THIRD LAYER:
1 pkg. instant chocolate fudge
    pudding
3 C. cold milk
1 pkg. instant French vanilla pudding

FOURTH LAYER:
1 to 2 C. whipped topping
Extra peanuts

Mix and press the first layer into a 9x13" pan. Bake at 350° for 15 minutes and cool.
Mix the second layer and spread on top of the first layer. Chill. Mix the third layer for 2
minutes and pour over the second layer. Top with whipped topping and peanuts.

Cupcake Cones

1/3 C. butter or margarine, softened
1/2 C. creamy peanut butter
1 1/2 C. packed brown sugar
2 eggs
1 tsp. vanilla extract

2 C. all-purpose flour
2 1/2 tsp. baking powder
1/2 tsp. salt
3/4 C. milk
Cake ice cream cones (about 3" tall)
Frosting of your choice

In a mixing bowl, cream butter, peanut butter and brown sugar. Beat in eggs and vanilla. Combine dry ingredients. Add to creamed mixture alternately with milk. Place ice cream cones in muffin cups. Spoon about 3 tablespoons batter into each cone, filling to 3/4" from the top. Bake at 350° for 25 to 30 minutes or until a toothpick inserted near center comes out clean. Frost and decorate as desired.

Peanut Butter Frosting

1/2 C. peanut butter
1 tsp. vanilla
1/4 C. butter

1/2 C. milk
4 1/2 C. powdered sugar

Mix all ingredients together until creamy.

Peanut Butter Caramel Bars

1 pkg. yellow cake mix
1/2 C. butter or margarine, softened
1 egg
20 miniature peanut butter cups, chopped
2 T. cornstarch

12 1/4 oz. jar caramel ice cream topping
1/4 C. peanut butter
1 C. salted peanuts
16 oz. can milk chocolate frosting

In a mixing bowl, combine dry cake mix, butter and egg; beat until no longer crumbly, about 3 minutes. Stir in the peanut butter cups. Press into greased 9x13x2" baking pan. Bake at 350° for 18 to 22 minutes or until lightly browned. Meanwhile, in a saucepan, combine cornstarch, caramel topping and peanut butter until smooth. Cook over low heat, stirring occasionally, until mixture comes to a boil, about 25 minutes. Cook and stir 1 to 2 minutes longer. Remove from heat and stir in 1/2 cup peanuts. Spread evenly over warm crust. Bake 6 to 7 minutes longer or until almost set. Cool completely on a wire rack. Spread with frosting. Sprinkle with 1/2 cup peanuts. Refrigerate for at least 1 hour before cutting. Store in the refrigerator.

Easter Cookie Nests

1 jar marshmallow creme
2 T. melted butter
3 C. (5 oz.) chow mein noodles

1/4 C. smooth peanut butter
1 C. crushed M & M's

Mix thoroughly. Refrigerate for 15 to 20 minutes. Grease hands and form nests. Place on wax paper and let dry.

Tumbleweeds

1-12 oz. can salted peanuts
1-7 oz. can potato sticks

3 C. butterscotch chips
3 T. peanut butter

Combine peanuts and potato sticks in a bowl, set aside. In a microwave, heat butterscotch chips and peanut butter for 1 to 2 minutes or until melted, stirring every 30 seconds. Add to peanut mixture. Stir to coat evenly. Drop by rounded tablespoonfuls onto waxed paper-lined baking sheets. Refrigerate until set, about 5 minutes.

Oatmeal Chocolate Chip
Peanut Butter Bars

1 C. sugar
2/3 C. brown sugar
1 C. softened butter
1 tsp. vanilla
1 C. peanut butter
2 eggs

2 C. flour
1 C. oatmeal
2 tsp. baking soda
1/4 tsp. salt
3/4 pkg. chocolate chips

Cream together sugar, brown sugar, butter, vanilla, peanut butter and eggs. Then add flour, oatmeal, baking soda, salt and chocolate chips. Mix well. Place in greased pan and bake for 20 minutes at 350°.

Peanut Butter Bars

1 stick margarine, melted
3/4 C. brown sugar
1/2 tsp. vanilla
2 C. peanut butter
1 lb. powdered sugar

TOPPING:
12 oz. pkg. chocolate chips, melted
2 T. butter
Small amount of hot water

Mix and melt ingredients. Press onto cookie sheet. Pat well with hands. Put waxed paper over top and roll with rolling pin until flat and smooth. Remove waxed paper and spread with topping. Cool and cut into squares

Monster Cookies

1/2 C. butter
1 C. sugar
1 C. plus 2 T. brown sugar
3 eggs, beaten
1 C. peanut butter
1/4 tsp. vanilla

3/4 tsp. light corn syrup
4 1/2 C. quick oats
2 tsp. baking soda
1/4 tsp. salt
1/2 lb. M & M's
6 oz. chocolate chips

Cream butter, gradually adding sugars; beat well. Add eggs, peanut butter, vanilla and corn syrup. Beat well. Add oats, soda and salt. Stir well. Add remaining ingredients and stir in. Drop dough by 1/4 cupfuls 4" apart on lightly greased cookie sheet. Bake at 325° for 15 minutes.

Peanut Blossoms

SIFT TOGETHER:
1 3/4 C. all-purpose flour
1 tsp. soda
1/2 tsp. salt
CREAM TOGETHER:
1/2 C. butter
1/2 C. peanut butter

GRADUALLY ADD:
1/2 C. sugar
1/2 C. firmly packed light brown
   sugar
CREAM WELL, THEN ADD:
1 unbeaten egg
1 tsp. vanilla

Beat well. Blend in the dry ingredients gradually; mix thoroughly. Shape dough into balls using a rounded teaspoonful for each. Roll balls in sugar and place on ungreased cookie sheets. Bake at 375° for 8 minutes. Remove sheet from oven and place a solid milk chocolate candy kiss on top of each cookie, pressing down firmly so that cookie cracks around the edge. Return cookie to oven and bake 2 to 5 minutes longer until brown.

Easy Peanut Blossoms

1-14 oz. can sweetened condensed
   milk
3/4 C. peanut butter

2 C. Bisquick baking mix
1 tsp. vanilla
Chocolate kisses

Beat milk and peanut butter. Add Bisquick and vanilla. Shape into balls, roll in granulated sugar. Bake at 350° for 6 to 8 minutes (do not over bake). Press a chocolate kiss on each, immediately after baking.

Chewey Surprise Cookies

1 1/2 C. butter flavored shortening	3 3/4 C. flour
1 1/2 C. peanut butter	2 tsp. soda
2 C. sugar, divided	1 1/2 tsp. baking powder
1 1/2 C. brown sugar, packed	3/4 tsp. salt
4 eggs	1-10 oz. pkg. Milk Duds

In a mixing bowl, cream shortening, peanut butter, 1 1/2 cups sugar and brown sugar. Add eggs, one at a time, beating well after each. Combine dry ingredients; gradually add to the creamed mixture. Chill for at least 1 hour. Shape 4 teaspoons of dough around each Milk Dud so it is completely covered. Roll balls in remaining sugar. Place on ungreased baking sheets. Bake at 350° for 10 to 12 minutes or until set. Cool for 5 minutes before removing to wire racks.

Peanut Butter Pie

1/3 C. peanut butter
3/4 C. powdered sugar
1/2 C. flour
1/2 C. sugar
3 egg yolks
3 T. butter

2 C. milk
1 tsp. vanilla
Pinch of salt
MERINGUE:
1/4 tsp. cream of tartar
3 egg whites

1 baked pie shell

Mix peanut butter and powdered sugar together. Save 1 tablespoon for on top of meringue. Put remaining in bottom of baked pie shell. Mix together flour, sugar, salt, a small amount of milk to moisten and egg yolks; beat well. Add milk and cook until thick. Add 3 tablespoons butter and 1 teaspoon vanilla. Pour mixture in pie shell. Beat 3 egg whites with 1/4 teaspoon cream of tartar until stiff. Put on pie. Top with peanut butter and powdered sugar. Bake 20 minutes at 350°.

Peanut Butter Cream Pie

1-8 oz. pkg. cream cheese, softened
3/4 C. confectioners' sugar
1/2 C. creamy peanut butter
6 T. milk

1-8 oz. carton whipped
  topping, thawed
1-9" graham cracker crust
1/4 C. peanuts, chopped

In a mixing bowl, beat cream cheese until fluffy. Add sugar and peanut butter; mix well. Carefully add the milk. Fold in whipped topping; spoon into the crust. Sprinkle with peanuts. Chill overnight.

Peanut Butter Cookies

1/2 C. margarine
1/2 C. peanut butter
1/2 C. granulated sugar
1/2 C. brown sugar, packed
1 egg

1 1/4 C. flour
1/2 tsp. baking powder
3/4 tsp. soda
1/4 tsp. salt

Preheat oven to 375°. Mix margarine, peanut butter, sugars and egg thoroughly. Blend all dry ingredients together; stir into peanut butter mixture. Roll dough into 1 1/4" balls. Place 3" apart on lightly greased baking sheet. Flatten crisscross style with fork dipped in flour. Bake 10 to 12 minutes.

No Bake Cookies

1/2 C. milk
1 stick butter
4 T. cocoa
2 C. sugar

1 tsp. vanilla
1/2 C. peanut butter
3 C. oatmeal

Mix first four ingredients and bring to a boil for 3 minutes. Remove from heat. Add vanilla, peanut butter and oatmeal. Drop by teaspoons on cookie sheets. Store in refrigerator.

Crunchy Kisses

1/2 C. white sugar
1/2 C. corn syrup

2/3 C. peanut butter
3 C. Cap'n Crunch cereal

Mix sugar and syrup in saucepan; bring to a boil over medium heat. Turn off heat and add peanut butter. Blend thoroughly with wooden spoon. Pour over Cap 'n Crunch in large bowl. Stir lightly until coated. Drop by tablespoonfuls onto waxed paper. Let cool.

Fudgy Buttons

2 T. butter or margarine
1 1/2 tsp. baking cocoa
1/2 C. confectioners' sugar

1/2 tsp. milk
2 T. creamy peanut butter

In a small saucepan, melt the butter; remove from the heat. Add cocoa and mix well. Stir in sugar. Add milk and stir until smooth. Add peanut butter and mix well. Drop by teaspoonfuls onto waxed paper; flatten tops and shape into 1" patties.

Cashew-Peanut Butter Fudge

1/2 C. peanut butter
1-12 oz. pkg. chocolate chips
1 C. cashews

1-11 oz. pkg. butterscotch chips
2 to 3 C. miniature marshmallows

Melt peanut butter and chips together. Add marshmallows and cashews. Pour into foil-lined buttered 9x9" pan. Let set. Very rich, so cut small.

Peanut Butter Temptations

1 C. butter or margarine, softened
1 C. brown sugar
1 C. sugar
1 C. peanut butter
2 eggs

2 tsp. vanilla
2 1/2 C. flour
1 1/2 tsp. soda
1 tsp. salt
72 miniature peanut butter cups

Cream together the first four ingredients. Add the eggs and vanilla and mix well. Blend all the ingredients together. Roll dough into 1" balls and place in an ungreased mini-muffin pan. Bake at 350° for 10 minutes. Remove from oven and press in miniature peanut butter cups until just the tops show. Let stand for 3 to 4 minutes before removing.

Butterscotch-Peanut Fudge

1-12 oz. pkg. butterscotch chips
1-14 oz. can sweetened condensed
   milk
1 1/2 C. miniature marshmallows

2/3 C. chunk-style peanut butter
1 tsp. vanilla
1 C. chopped peanuts
Dash of salt

In saucepan, combine butterscotch chips, milk and marshmallows. Stir over medium heat until marshmallows melt. Remove from heat; beat in peanut butter, vanilla and dash of salt. Stir in nuts. Pour in buttered 9x9x2" pan. Chill. Cut in squares. Store in refrigerator. Makes 4 dozen squares.

Poppy Seed Cookies

1 C. margarine
1/2 C. sugar
2 egg yolks
2 C. flour
1/4 tsp. salt

1/4 C. poppy seeds
3/4 tsp. baking powder
3/4 C. chocolate chips
1/4 C. peanut butter

Cream margarine, sugar and egg; blend in flour, salt, poppy seeds and baking powder. Chill. Shape into 1" balls and place on greased cookie sheets, 1" apart. Make a depression in center of each ball with thumb. Bake at 375° for about 10 minutes. Cool. Melt chocolate chips and peanut butter together; fill depressions with this mixture.

Peanut Butter Bars

1/2 C. butter, softened
1/2 C. sugar
1/2 C. brown sugar
1/2 C. creamy peanut butter
1 egg, beaten
1 tsp. vanilla

1 C. flour
1/2 C. quick-cooking oats
1 tsp. baking soda
1/4 tsp. salt
1 C. semisweet chocolate chips

ICING:
1/2 C. powdered sugar
2 T. creamy peanut butter

2 T. milk

In a mixing bowl, cream butter, sugars and peanut butter. Add egg and vanilla; mix well. Combine flour, oats, baking soda and salt; stir into the creamed mixture. Spread into a greased 9x13" baking pan. Sprinkle with chocolate chips. Bake at 350° for 20 to 25 minutes. Combine icing ingredients; drizzle over bars.

Chocolate Peanut Butter Bars

2 1/2 C. powdered sugar
2 C. graham cracker crumbs
1 C. peanut butter

1 C. margarine, melted
12 oz. pkg. chocolate chips

Mix sugar and crumbs together with peanut butter. Add melted margarine and mix. Pat firmly in 9x13" pan. Melt chocolate chips and spread on top. Refrigerate until firm. Cut into bars.

Almond Bark Cookies

1 lb. white almond bark
1 C. chunky peanut butter
1 C. cocktail peanuts

1 C. Rice Krispies
1 C. mini-marshmallows

Melt and stir almond bark in crock pot. Turn off when melted and stir well. Add chunky peanut butter; stir well. Add cocktail peanuts, Rice Krispies and mini-marshmallows. Mix well and drop by teaspoons on waxed paper.

Peanutty Chocolate Snack Squares

5 graham crackers, broken into
   squares
1/2 C. sugar
1 C. light corn syrup

1 C. chocolate chips
1 C. peanut butter
1 C. dry roasted peanuts

Line bottom of an 8" square pan with graham cracker squares, cutting to fit if necessary. In a 2-quart microwave-safe bowl, stir together sugar and corn syrup. Microwave at high, stirring every 2 minutes, until mixture boils, boil 3 minutes. Stir in chocolate chips, peanut butter and peanuts. Pour over crackers; spread carefully. Cover and refrigerate until firm. Cut into 2" squares. Refrigerate leftovers.

Crunchy Fudge Sandwiches

1 C. (6 oz. pkg.) butterscotch morsels
1/2 C. peanut butter
4 C. Rice Krispies
1 T. water

1 C. (6 oz. pkg.) chocolate morsels
1/2 C. sugar
2 T. butter, softened

Melt butterscotch morsels with peanut butter in saucepan over low heat, stirring until well blended. Remove from heat. Add Rice Krispies, stir until well coated. Press half of cereal mixture into buttered 8x8x2" pan. Chill in refrigerator, while preparing for fudge mixture. Set remaining cereal aside. Combine chocolate morsels, sugar, butter and water in top of double boiler, place over hot water. Stir until chocolate melts and mixture is well blended. Spread over chilled cereal mixture. Spread remaining cereal mixture evenly over top. Press gently! Chill! Remove from refrigerator for about 10 minutes.

Chocolate Marshmallow Crisps

1 C. semisweet chocolate chips
1/4 C. peanut butter

3 C. crispy rice cereal
1 C. miniature marshmallows

In microwave-safe bowl, melt chocolate chips and peanut butter. In a medium bowl, put cereal and marshmallows,. Pour melted chocolate mixture over and mix well. Place in a well greased 8x8x2" pan.

Scotch Rice Krispie Bars

6 C. Rice Krispies
1 C. sugar
1 C. light corn syrup

1 C. peanut butter
1 C. chocolate chips
1 C. butterscotch chips

Bring sugar and syrup to a boil. Remove from heat and add peanut butter. Add Rice Krispies and pat in a 9x13" pan. Melt chips and spread over bars.

Cracker Goodies

3 1/2 C. powdered sugar
1 1/4 C. graham crackers, crushed
1 C. peanut butter

1/2 C. margarine
1 C. chocolate chips

Mix powdered sugar and graham cracker crumbs together. Pour melted margarine on this; add peanut butter and mix. Put in 9x13" pan. Pour melted chocolate chips on top.

Peanut Bars

1 C. sugar
1 C. dark corn syrup
1 C. peanut butter
1 tsp. vanilla

4 C. corn flakes
2 C. sugar coated corn cereal
1 C. salted Spanish peanuts

Bring sugar and corn syrup to a boil. Remove from heat. Add peanut butter and vanilla. Mix well. Then add corn flakes, puffed corn cereal and salted peanuts. Spread in a buttered 9x13" pan. Cool and cut into squares.

Hop Scotch Candy

1/2 C. peanut butter
1-6 oz. pkg. butterscotch chips
2 C. chow mein noodles

2 C. miniature marshmallows
1 C. nuts or peanuts

In top of double boiler, combine peanut butter and butterscotch chips. Place over hot, but not boiling water and stir until melted and blended. Add noodles, marshmallows and nuts, stirring to coat. Drop by teaspoonfuls onto waxed paper-lined cookie sheet.

Peanut Butter Easter Eggs

8 oz. cream cheese, softened
1 stick butter, softened
18 oz. jar smooth peanut butter

2 lbs. powdered sugar
2 tsp. vanilla
2 lbs. melted chocolate

Mix cream cheese and butter by hand. Add peanut butter, powdered sugar and vanilla. Chill overnight. Shape into eggs. Coat with 2 pounds of melted chocolate.

Peanut Butter Bon Bons

1 stick margarine
1 lb. powdered sugar
2 C. peanut butter

3 C. Rice Krispies
Chocolate almond bark, melted

Mix margarine, powdered sugar, peanut butter and Rice Krispies. Form into balls (about 1 teaspoon each). Chill the balls. Dip into melted almond bark. These freeze well.

Peanut Butter Oatmeal Chip Cookies

1 1/2 C. margarine, softened	1 1/2 tsp. soda
1 1/2 C. white sugar	1 tsp. salt
1 1 /2 C. brown sugar	1 1/2 tsp. vanilla
1/2 C. peanut butter	1/2 tsp. baking powder
3 eggs	3 C. rolled oatmeal
2 3/4 C. flour	Chocolate chips, M & M's, butterscotch chips

Cream margarine, white sugar, brown sugar and peanut butter. Add eggs. Add flour, soda, salt, vanilla and baking powder. Stir. Add oatmeal. Stir. Add chocolate chips, M & M's and butterscotch chips and stir again. Can be chilled overnight. Drop by teaspoonfuls onto lightly greased cookie sheets. Bake at 350° for 8 to 10 minutes until golden around edges.

Peanutty Chocolate Pudding

2 C. cold milk   1/2 C. peanut butter
1-1.4 oz. pkg. instant chocolate pudding

In a mixing bowl, combine milk and pudding mix. Beat on low speed for 2 minutes. Beat in peanut butter until smooth. Spoon into dessert dishes. Top with whipped topping if desired.

Chocolate Peanut Buddy Bars

1 C. peanut butter
6 T. butter, softened
1 1/4 C. sugar
3 eggs

1 tsp. vanilla
1 C. flour
1/4 tsp. salt
11 1/2 oz. bag chocolate chips,
 divided

Preheat oven to 350°. In a large mixing bowl, beat peanut butter and butter until smooth. Add sugar, eggs and vanilla, beat until creamy. Gradually beat in flour and salt. Stir in 1 cup chocolate chips and spread into greased 9x13" pan. Bake 25 to 30 minutes until edges are brown. Immediately sprinkle remaining chocolate chips over cookie layer. Let stand 5 minutes to melt, then spread over top. Cool before serving.

Deluxe Chocolate Marshmallow Bars

3/4 C. butter, softened
1 1/2 C. sugar
3 eggs
1 tsp. vanilla
1 1/3 C. flour
3 T. cocoa
1/2 tsp. baking powder
1/2 tsp. salt
4 C. mini-marshmallows

TOPPING:
1 1/3 C. chocolate chips
1 C. peanut butter
3 T. butter
2 C. Rice Krispies

Cream butter and sugars. Add eggs and vanilla, beat until fluffy. Add flour, baking powder, salt and cocoa. Spread in a greased pan. Bake at 350° for 15 to 18 minutes. Sprinkle marshmallows even over cake, return to oven for 2 to 3 minutes. Using a knife dipped in water, spread marshmallows evenly. Cool.
TOPPING: Combine chocolate chips, peanut butter and butter. Cook over low heat. Remove from heat, add cereal. Spread over bars. Chill.

Crunchy Graham Bars

1 C. sugar
1 C. white corn syrup

1 C. peanut butter
6 C. Golden Grahams cereal

Boil sugar and syrup for 30 seconds. Add peanut butter and stir well. Pour mixture over cereal. Mix well. Pat into a buttered 9x13" pan. Cut into bars when cool.

Cookie Ice Cream Sandwiches

Peanut butter
12 oatmeal raisin cookies

1 pt. vanilla ice cream or flavor of
   your choice
Miniature chocolate chips

Spread peanut butter over the bottom of six cookies. Top with a scoop of ice cream. Top with another cookie; press down gently. Roll side of ice cream sandwich in chocolate chips. Wrap in plastic wrap. Freeze until serving.

Peanut Butter Cup Cupcakes

1/3 C. shortening
1/3 C. peanut butter
1 1/4 C. brown sugar
2 eggs
1 tsp. vanilla

1 3/4 C. flour
1 3/4 tsp. baking powder
1 C. milk
16 peanut butter cups

Cream shortening, peanut butter and brown sugar. Add eggs and vanilla, mix well. Combine flour and baking powder, add to creamed mixture alternately with milk. Fill muffin cups 1/4 cup full. Press peanut butter cup into center until top is even with batter. Bake at 350° for 22 to 24 minutes.

Drumstick Bars

2 C. vanilla wafers, crushed
1/2 C. butter or margarine, melted
1 C. crushed salted peanuts
1-8 oz. pkg. cream cheese, softened
1/3 C. peanut butter

1 C. powdered sugar
4 C. whipped topping
2 small pkgs. instant chocolate
   pudding
3 C. milk
1 large chocolate bar

FIRST LAYER: Mix crushed vanilla wafers, melted butter and 2/3 cup of the crushed peanuts. Put in a 9x13" pan. Bake at 350° for 10 minutes.
SECOND LAYER: Mix cream cheese, peanut butter and powdered sugar until smooth. Fold in 2 cups whipped topping. Spread over first layer.
THIRD LAYER: Mix chocolate pudding and milk. Chill to set. Spread over second layer.
FOURTH LAYER: Spread 2 cups whipped topping over third layer. Sprinkle 1/3 cup of the chopped peanuts over top. Grate chocolate bar and sprinkle over top. Chill overnight.

M & M Bars

2 C. oatmeal
1 C. brown sugar
1/2 tsp. salt
1 can sweetened condensed milk
1 C. M & M's

1 1/2 C. flour
1 tsp. baking soda
1 C. melted butter
1/3 C. peanut butter

Combine oats, flour, sugar, soda and salt, mix well. Add butter, mix until dry ingredients are thoroughly moistened and mixture resembles coarse crumbs. Reserve 1 1/2 cups crumb mixture. Press remaining crumbs into the bottom of a greased 9x13" pan. Bake at 375° for 12 minutes. Combine condensed milk and peanut butter in small mixing bowl, mixing until well blended. Spread over partially baked crust within 1/4" from edge. Combine reserved crumbs and M & M's. Sprinkle evenly over sweetened condensed milk mixture and press lightly. Continue baking 20 to 22 minutes or until golden brown.

Chocolate Wheat Wafers

Wheat Thin crackers
Peanut butter

1/2 pkg. chocolate almond bark
6 oz. chocolate chips

Make sandwiches of two Wheat Thin crackers spread with peanut butter. Dip in coating **of melted almond bark** combined with chocolate chips.

Index

Appetizers

Main Dish

Desserts